INTRODUC

What do Avocados and Pineapples have in common? They both control blood pressure, they are both excellent digestive aids, they aid in skin cleansing keeps your cholesterol levels healthy! But they also have their differences too and it is best to tap into both the detox benefits of avocados and the anti-inflammatory properties of pineapples with a special Fruitilicious bundle featuring 50 Super Delicious Avocado and Pineapple Recipes!

This magnificent set of two cookbooks provides access to a multitude of appetizers, salads, main course meals and desserts. Add a new dimension of flavor by making Avocado Bomb Sauce or go directly vegan with Avocado Chickpea Pesto. Add zest to your seafood dishes by making a delicious Salmon Pineapple Meal or go for the downright fancy with a delightful Pineapple Cheese Casserole!

Add some avocados and pineapples in your daily routines and you'll never go back!

The Magnificent Avocado Cookbook: 25 Splendid Recipes for Any Taste

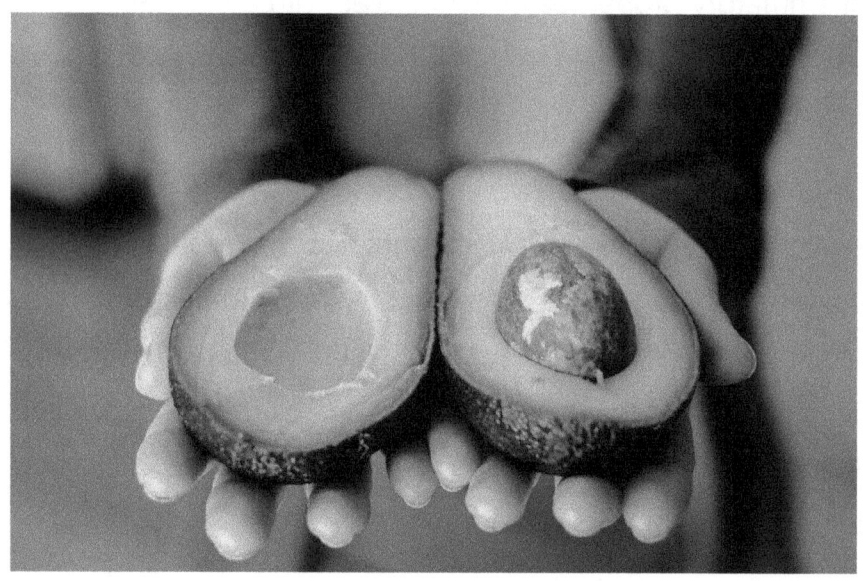

INTRODUCTION 1
INTRODUCTION 8
CHAPTER 1: APPETIZERS AND DIPS WITH AVOCADO 9
   Crispy baked avocado fries 10
   Avocado egg rolls with sweet chili sauce 13
   Sweet potato guacamole bacon bites 16
   Avocado dip with corn 19
   Avocado bomb sauce 21
   Creamy avocado ranch dip 24
   The ultimate green avocado spinach dip 27
CHAPTER 2: SALADS AND VEGAN MEALS WITH AVOCADO 30
   Avocado and three bean salad 31
   Avocado tuna salad 34
   Avocado egg salad 36
   Cucumber, tomato and avocado salad 38
   Vegan potato salad with cilantro and dill 40
   Avocado Chickpea with vegan pesto 43
   Black bean salad with avocado cilantro- lime juice 45
CHAPTER 3: MAIN COURSE MEALS WITH AVOCADO 48
   Steak and sweet potato bowls with avocado cilantro drizzle 48
   Stuffed avocado tacos 54
   Greek meatballs with Avocado Tzatziki sauce 57
   Avocado Caprese skillet chicken 60
   Pan-seared salmon with creamy avocado sauce 63
   Avocado and lump crab 66
CHAPTER 4: DESSERTS AND SMOOTHIES WITH AVOCADO 69
   Avocado and banana ice-cream 69

Paleo chocolate mousse 72

Avocado brownies 75

Pineapple Avocado ultimate green smoothie 78

Layered avocado and strawberry smoothie 80

Introduction 86

Chapter 1: Delicious Pineapple Smoothies & Breakfasts 88

Morning Pineapple Flax 88

Pineapple Egg Toast 90

Morning Pineapple Oat Granola Mix 92

Truly Tropical Mango Pineapple Smoothie 94

Pineapple Orange Smoothie 96

Pineapple Honey Peach Smoothie 97

Chapter 2: Fresh Pineapple Meals & Salads 99

Wholesome Pineapple Avocado Corn Salad 99

Fruity Pineapple Yogurt Salad 101

Pork Pineapple Rice Treat 103

Pineapple Berry Kale Salad 105

Pineapple Mayo Chicken Salad 107

Pineapple Glazed Pork Roast 109

Salmon Pineapple Meal 112

BBQ Pineapple Chicken 114

Chapter 3: Popular Pinelicious Recipes 116

Pineapple Perky Sandwich 116

Pineapple Rum Relish 118

Pineapple Tortilla Pizza 120

Shrimp Pineapple Zucchini Curry 122

Cinnamon Pineapple Bites 124

Chapter 4: Awesome Pineapple Desserts 126

- Pineapple Cream Cake 126
- Pineapple Ginger Sorbet 128
- Pineapple Marshmallow Fluff 130
- Pineapple Dessert Cookies 132
- Pineapple Cheese Casserole 134
- Pineapple Fruit Freeze 136

Conclusion 138

INTRODUCTION

Avocado is simply an inimitable fruit from any point of view! It is super delicious, and it can be used in any meal, from yummy dips to mouthwatering desserts. It is healthy, as it contains great quantities of monosaturated fats, which are vital for proper nutrition and body-functioning in general. It is a super-food as well, as besides good fats, avocado has plenty of other nutrients and vitamins to offer

The Magnificent Avocado Cookbook focuses on showing you how to make delicious meals with avocados, we will make dips, salads, rolls, desserts and smoothies, and even bake avocados. This fruit will become your favorite food, believe me!

Let our amazing culinary journey begin!

CHAPTER 1: APPETIZERS AND DIPS WITH AVOCADO

Have you ever prepared avocado appetizers? You may have seen these on restaurant menus but never had the guts to try making on your own? This is your chance to make them in your own kitchen, and you will wonder why you had not tried them out sooner.

The dips are a must-have in your pantry. They go well with chips, or you can even use them as dressing.

Crispy baked avocado fries

There is nothing more fulfilling than discovering healthier ways to fill up on your favorite snacks. Fries just got a whole lot healthier if you are using avocado. You can serve your guests or family as an appetizer as you prepare the main meal. It works perfectly.

Preparation time: 20 minutes

Serves: 4

Ingredients:

- Ripe avocados pitted and sliced – 3
- Egg, slightly beaten – 2
- Freshly squeezed lime juice – 2 tablespoons
- Extra virgin olive oil – 3 tablespoons
- Flour of your choice (I prefer whole-wheat) – ½ cup
- Bread crumbs – 1 ½ cups
- Kosher salt and black pepper to taste

Method:

- Preheat your oven to 400 degrees F
- Line your baking tray with nonstick spray and set aside
- Season your avocado slices with lime juice, salt, and pepper. This preserves their color and flavor while baking

- Coat your seasoned slices with flour and then dip each slice in the slightly beaten egg
- Finally, evenly coat the slices with the breadcrumbs and bake for 15 minutes or until the avocado slices are crispy
- Take it out from the oven then serve with your favorite dipping sauce

Avocado egg rolls with sweet chili sauce

There are many various ways of preparing egg rolls. These are a must-make in my house every week, and when I realized I could add avocados to the otherwise popular egg rolls, I was delighted. You will be happy too when you try this recipe out.

The egg rolls are a perfect appetizer because they are crunchy and light leaving you with just enough space to enjoy your main meal.

Preparation time: 15 minutes

Serves: 4

Ingredients:

- Egg roll wrappers – 8
- Ripe avocados pitted and sliced – 3
- Roma tomatoes, nicely diced – 2
- Kosher salt and pepper to taste
- Canola oil for deep frying
- For the sweet chili sauce
- White sugar – 1 ½ tablespoons
- Rice vinegar – 1 tablespoon
- Sriracha – 4 tablespoons
- Sesame oil -1 tablespoon

Method:

- Combine the sliced avocados, diced tomato, kosher salt and black pepper in a large bowl. Mix until you get a uniform consistency
- Add all the sauce ingredients in another smaller bowl and mix well
- Lay out the egg roll wrappers and evenly transfer your avocado mixture to each wrapper

- Use water to brush up all four edges of the wrappers. Start by folding the corners over your avocado filling and then the sides of all wrappers
- Heat your canola oil over high heat in a large pan. The oil should be about 2 inches thick
- When the oil is 350 F or starts to smoke, add your egg rolls in batches and fry until golden brown
- Move the cooked egg rolls onto a paper towel to drain the oil and Cut each egg roll diagonally
- Serve while still warm with the chili sauce

Sweet potato guacamole bacon bites

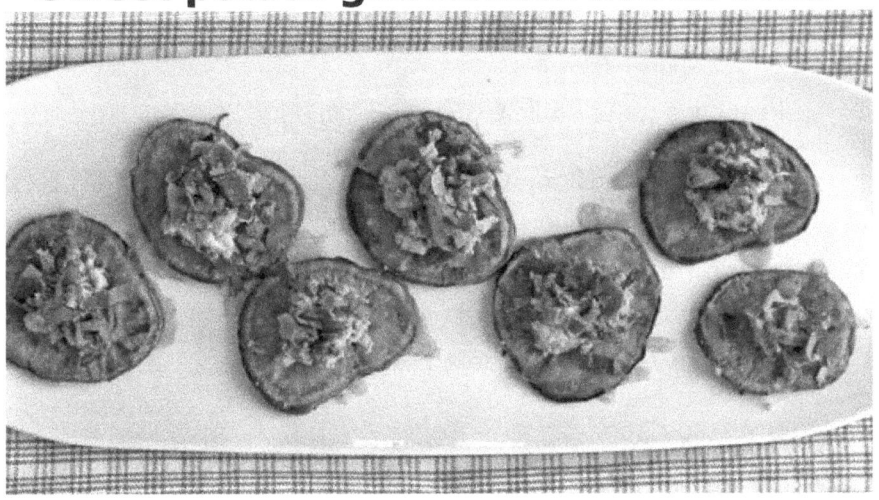

The sweetness of potatoes and creaminess from avocados makes this one of my favorite appetizers. They are so good that you will always want to make the bites for a picnic or when visiting a friend's house.

Preparation time: 35 minutes

Serves: 5

Ingredients:

For the guacamole

- Ripe avocados, peeled and sliced – 4
- Roma tomato, nicely chopped – 2

- Garlic, crushed – 2 cloves
- Red onions, chopped – 2
- Freshly squeezed lime juice – 3 tablespoons
- Kosher salt and pepper to taste

For the bacon bites

- Large sweet potato, peeled and thinly sliced – 2
- Smoked bacon strips – 5
- Guacamole – 3 cups
- Sweet red onion, thinly sliced – 1
- Extra virgin olive oil – 2 tablespoons
- Kosher salt and pepper to taste
- Hot sauce of your choice

Method:

- Add all the guacamole ingredients in a large bowl and mix until you attain a thick uniform mixture. Set aside
- Combine your sliced sweet potato, olive oil, kosher salt and black pepper in a large bowl
- Preheat your oven to 300 degrees F and line your baking tray with non-stick spray

- Line your seasoned sweet potato slices on the baking sheet and bake for 25 minutes or until they become golden brown. Remove from the oven and set aside
- Cook your bacon slices in a medium sized skillet and reserve one tablespoon of the bacon grease
- Use the reserved bacon grease to cook the onions until they become transparent
- Dice the cooked bacon and set aside together with the fried onions to cool
- Scoop your guacamole and use as a topping for your cooled sweet potato slices
- Top this with the cooked onion and sliced bacon
- Garnish with your favorite hot sauce and serve. Enjoy!

Avocado dip with corn

There is nothing like a nice twist to your go-to avocado dip. The corn is an exciting addition that gives the avocado dip a fabulous look and an even greater taste that even your pickiest eaters will want to try.

This dip can be made and refrigerated ready to be scooped up for a barbecue, a picnic or just a lazy day at home.

Preparation time: 10 minutes

Serves: 4

Ingredients:

- Ripe avocados, peeled and diced – 4
- Corn, drained – 1 cup

- Black beans washed and well drained – 1 cup
- green onions, nicely chopped – 3
- Green salsa Verde – 1 cup
- Cilantro

Method:

- Mix your avocados, black beans, corn and red onion in a large bowl
- Stir in your salsa Verde and keep mixing until it forms a uniform thick and creamy mixture
- Serve and enjoy with some tortilla chips or store in the refrigerator for later use

Avocado bomb sauce

The title speaks for itself. This avocado sauce is super fantastic. It's creamy, with a consistency and spicy taste to die for. I love making my avocado sauce ahead of time and storing it in the refrigerator in mason jars. It can be used whenever I feel like it. Which, is almost all the time, because the sauce goes with just about anything.

Preparation time: 10 minutes

Serves: 6

Ingredients:

- Large ripe avocados, peeled and sliced – 3
- Fresh cilantro, rinsed and drained - 1 cup
- Extra virgin oil – ¼ cup
- Fresh Jalapeno - 1
- Garlic, crushed – 3 cloves
- Freshly squeezed lime juice – ¾ cup
- Kosher salt – 1 tablespoon
- Water (optional)– 1 cup

Method:

- Mix all your components in a food processor or a blender.
- Blend until you reach your desired thick consistency
- If you want a much thinner sauce, you can keep adding water until you attain your desired consistency
- Transfer your avocado mixture to a mason jar and serve.
- Enjoy with salads, egg rolls, and steaks or with just about anything else you have in mind.

Creamy avocado ranch dip

Whenever you want to go fancy with your dips, this ranch dip should be your first pick. The avocados bring a healthy option to the table making this among the tastiest and nutritious dips we have out there.

This can work whether you are having friends over for a game day, or you want to impress your guests with a great appetizer. This is the perfect dip to go with it.

Preparation time: 10 minutes

Serves: 5

Ingredients:

- Ripe avocados, peeled and sliced – 4
- Cherry tomatoes, pulpless and chopped – 1 cup
- Sour cream – 1 cup
- Greek yogurt – ¾ cup
- Buttermilk – ¼ cup
- Kosher salt and black pepper to taste
- Onion powder – 1 tablespoon
- Spring onions, rinsed and chopped – ¼ cup
- Small Green chili pepper – 1
- Small Red Bell Pepper - 1
- Fresh cilantro, chopped – ½ cup
- Garlic powder – 2 tablespoons
- Black peppercorns, crushed – 1 tablespoon

Method:

- While using a large bowl, mix your sour cream, Greek yogurt, buttermilk, onion and garlic powder, kosher salt and crushed peppercorn until you get a creamy mixture
- In a different bowl, mash your avocados and stir in your tomatoes, cilantro and green and red pepper

- Shift the avocado blend to the bowl with the ranch dressing
- Mix slowly until you attain a thick uniform consistency
- Serve and enjoy with tortilla chips or a side of your choice.

The ultimate green avocado spinach dip

I love greens. And so should you. They are laden with antioxidants that shield our bodies from so many diseases.

So when I got a chance to mix two of my favorite things; avocado and spinach, I could not pass that up. The dip has a creamy texture and a remarkable taste. You just have to try it out to see what I'm talking about.

Preparation time: 10 minutes

Serves: 4

Ingredients:

- Large avocados, peeled and thinly sliced – 2
- Fresh spinach, rinsed and shredded – 2 cups
- Low-fat sour cream – 1/2 cup
- Red onion, diced – 1
- Garlic, chopped – 2 cloves
- Freshly squeezed lime juice – 2 tablespoons
- Jalapeno pepper, chopped – 1
- Hot sauce of your choice

Method:

- Mix all your ingredients in a food processor or blender
- Combine until you get a thick cream texture
- Transfer your mixture to a large bowl, cover with plastic wrap and store in your refrigerator until you are ready to serve

CHAPTER 2: SALADS AND VEGAN MEALS WITH AVOCADO

I believe all salads should be light and tasty. Why? There is a reason you go for a salad and not the main meal. You want something light that will also fill you up.

Salads are perfect for lunch when you do not have much time, or you want to eat in your office. If you are vegan I have vegan options for you that are just as delightful.

Avocado and three bean salad

The key factor that you will notice first about this salad is how vibrant the colors are. You will love it! This salad will quickly become a favorite in your home because it has a great taste. Moreover, it can be used as a side dish or as a light option for either lunch or dinner.

Preparation time: 60 minutes

Serves: 4

Ingredients:

- Ripe avocados, peeled and sliced – 2
- Black beans, well rinsed and drained – 8 oz
- Red kidney beans, well rinsed and drained – 8 oz
- Garbanzo beans, well rinsed and drained – 8 oz
- Extra virgin olive oil – ¼ cup
- Fresh cilantro, chopped – 1 cup
- Red bell pepper, diced – 1
- Cherry tomatoes, cubed – 2
- Freshly squeezed lime juice – 2 tablespoons
- Garlic, crushed – 2 cloves
- Kosher salt and pepper to taste

Method:

- coat your avocado with the lime juice to preserve its color throughout the process
- combine all your ingredients in a large bowl and store in your refrigerator for 50 minutes or until you are ready to eat
- Serve and enjoy!

Avocado tuna salad

The combination of avocado and tuna has some simply amazing health benefits to offer due to high contents of monosaturated fats in both ingredients! Its tasty, light and so healthy! You've simply got to try this out.

Preparation time: 5 minutes

Serves: 4

Ingredients:

- Large ripe avocado, peeled and sliced – 1
- Canned tuna, soaked in olive oil and drained – 12 oz

- Extra virgin olive oil – ½ cup
- Celery, minced – ¼ cup
- Freshly squeezed lemon juice – 3 tablespoons
- Fresh cilantro or parsley to garnish – 1 cup
- Kosher salt and black pepper to taste

Method:

- Combine all your ingredients in a large bowl and mix until well mixed. The avocado should be all mashed up and the tuna cut in tiny chunks
- Garnish with your cilantro or parsley and serve

Avocado egg salad

There is a million ways to enjoy our eggs. But you should definitely try this version too, and I am confident, you will fall in love with its delicate taste!

Preparation time: 15 minutes

Serves: 4

Ingredients:

- Ripe avocados, peeled and well mashed – 2
- Hard boiled eggs – 6
- Freshly squeezed lime juice – 2 tablespoons
- Kosher salt and pepper to taste

- Green onion to garnish

Method:

- Start by peeling and dicing your already boiled eggs
- Combine your avocado, lemon juice, salt, and pepper in a large bowl and mix well
- Stir in your diced eggs and keep mixing until you attain your desired consistency
- Garnish with green onions.
- Serve over your favorite pastry

Enjoy!

Cucumber, tomato and avocado salad

I can easily acknowledge that this is the easiest salad I have ever come across. You already have the ingredients in your pantry. What are you waiting for? It's time to whip up a healthy and sumptuous veg salad.

Preparation time: 10 minutes

Serves: 4

Ingredients:

- Ripe avocados, peeled and sliced – 2
- Roma tomatoes, washed and diced – 1 cup
- Large English cucumber, nicely chopped – 1
- Red onion, chopped – 1
- Extra virgin olive oil – 2 tablespoons
- Fresh dill, chopped – ¼ cup
- Kosher salt and pepper to taste
- Freshly squeezed lime juice – 3 tablespoons

Method:

- Combine all your vegetables in a large salad bowl and mix well
- Sprinkle your olive oil, salt, pepper and lime juice and toss gently
- Serve and enjoy!

Vegan potato salad with cilantro and dill

Sometimes going for an all vegan meal is quite the task. You have to go an extra mile to make the dish delicious and healthy at the same time. Well, this recipe is not one of the hard ones. It's simple, definitely vegan and best of all, I didn't use any mayo for the salad. You can use the herbs of your liking. It's a delish!

Preparation time: 40 minutes

Serves: 3

Ingredients:

- Ripe avocado, peeled and sliced – 1 ½
- Potatoes, peeled and diced – 5
- Fresh cilantro and dill, chopped - 1 cup
- Freshly squeezed lime juice – 2 tablespoons
- Kosher salt and black pepper to taste

Method:

- Start by boiling your potatoes in salty water for about 10 minutes or until they are tender
- Store in the freezer to cool for about 30 minutes (you want them a bit crispy)
- While the potatoes are cooling, combine the rest of your ingredients in a large bowl and mix well. Set aside
- When the potatoes are ready, remove from freezer and add them to the bowl. Give one last mix and serve.

Enjoy!

Avocado Chickpea with vegan pesto

If you are vegan or just love vegan foods, this will be such a treat for you. The vegan pesto is a hoot, but you can always choose any other gluten free dressing for this recipe. It's easy to make, healthy and of course, super delicious.

Preparation time: 10 minutes

Serves: 4

Ingredients:

- Ripe avocados, peeled and cubed – 2
- Chickpeas, well rinsed and drained – 1 can
- Spring mix or baby arugula, chopped – ½ cup

- Freshly squeezed lime juice – 2 tablespoons
- Scallions, rinsed and chopped (optional)
- Vegan basil arugula pesto – 4 tablespoons
- Kosher salt and pepper to taste

Method:

- Coat your avocado with the lime juice to preserve its color
- Add all your ingredients in a large bowl and mix until well combined
- Serve and enjoy!

Black bean salad with avocado cilantro-lime juice

If you haven't had a black bean salad by now, you are clearly missing out. This recipe is packed with a whole lot of nutrition, flavor and tastes even better than it looks. It will only make you 10 minutes to make this. I don't know what you are waiting for.

Preparation time: 10 minutes

Serves: 4

Ingredients:

- Ripe avocados, peeled and diced – 2
- Black beans, well rinsed and drained – 12 oz
- Garlic, crushed – 2 cloves
- Red bell peppers, thinly diced -2
- Extra virgin oil – 3 tablespoons
- Shallots, well minced – 2 tablespoons
- Cayenne pepper – ½ teaspoon
- Sugar – 1 teaspoon
- Lime zest – 1 tablespoon
- Freshly squeezed lime juice – 2 tablespoons
- Fresh cilantro or parsley to garnish – ½ cup
- Kosher salt and black pepper to taste

Method:

- Add all your ingredients except the avocados in a large bowl
- Mix gently and store in the refrigerator overnight. Always use an airtight container or a ziplock bag
- When ready to serve, add your avocados to the black bean mixture and toss gently. Do not mash the avocados
- Garnish with fresh cilantro or parsley, and it is ready to be served.

CHAPTER 3: MAIN COURSE MEALS WITH AVOCADO

This is my favorite thing to do with my avocados. I experiment them with different main course dishes, and the result is always fantastic. Give it a try today, and I promise, you will not be disappointed.

Steak and sweet potato bowls with avocado cilantro drizzle

What I liked most about this recipe is that its gluten and dairy free. You will get a colorful meal out of this recipe that even your picky kids will want to try.

With it being the main course meal, there is a lot that goes into it, but it's one big simple step to making the dish of your dreams.

Preparation time: 1 hour

Serves: 4

Ingredients:

- Large ripe avocado, sliced into bits – 1
- Steak (your choice) – 2 lb.
- Sweet potato, peeled and cubed – 1
- Kale, shredded – 2 cups
- Extra virgin olive oil – 2 tablespoons
- Garlic, chopped – 2 cloves
- Kosher salt and ground black pepper to examine
- Cooked rice to serve – 2 cups

For the cilantro drizzle

- Ripe avocado – 1
- Cilantro, packed – ½ cup
- Lime juice – 2 tablespoons
- Garlic, chopped – 2 cloves

- Kosher salt and pepper to taste

For steak marinade

- Gluten free soy sauce or tamari – ½ cup
- Extra virgin olive oil – 2 tablespoons
- Garlic, crushed – 4 cloves
- Ginger, ground – 1 teaspoon
- Red pepper flakes – 1 teaspoon

Method:

- Start off with the marinade to make the rest of the recipe an easy one. Combine all the marinade ingredients and add to the steak. Store refrigerated overnight or for 6 hours for best results
- As the steak marinates, preheat your oven to 425 degrees F
- Line your baking sheet with non-stick spray and add the sweet potato
- Drizzle the extra virgin oil on the sweet potato and season with kosher salt, black pepper, and crushed garlic
- Coat the potatoes evenly and proceed to bake for up to 30 minutes, stirring after 15 minutes. The sweet potatoes should be a golden brown by now

- Using a large skillet, add your extra virgin olive oil and heat over medium- high heat
- Add your marinated steak at this point, searing each side for about 3 minutes each. This is for medium-rare steaks. For medium-well steaks, leave on the pan for a bit longer. Let them sit on a cutting board for approximately 10 minutes before you start cutting them into strips against the grain
- To get the perfect avocado-cilantro dressing, add all your dressing ingredients to a blender or food processor and blend until smooth. Keep adding water at intervals until it attains your desired consistency
- Add kosher salt, lime juice, and pepper to the dressing to get your desired taste
- Serve your cooked rice in bowls then top with the steak, roasted sweet potatoes, sliced avocado and kale and finally avocado-cilantro dressing.

Enjoy!

Stuffed avocado tacos

This has to be among the simplest meals that you can just whip up on a lazy day. The tacos are pretty easy to make, and the avocados give them a perfect finish.

The first time I tried this, my avocado halves kept tipping over in the oven until I realized you could cut out some part of the avocado bottom so that it finally stops tipping.

Preparation time: 30 minutes

Serves: 6

Ingredients:

- Ripe avocados pitted and halved – 4
- Beef, Ground – 2 lb.
- Onion, shredded– 1 lb.
- Tomato, well diced – 1
- Mexican cheese, grated – 1 cup
- Taco seasoning – 2oz.
- Sour cream – ½ cup
- Cilantro to garnish – 1 cup
- Water – ¾ cup

Method:

- Preheat your oven to 350 degrees F
- In the meantime, brown your ground beef in a large pan. Drain any excess grease
- Stir in water, taco seasoning and your onion.
- When the onions start changing color, remove the pan from heat
- Scoop some avocado from the middle to make room for the taco mixture. The avocado you scoop out should be mixed with the mixture in the pan together with the diced tomato

- Now transfer the meat mixture to the avocado and top up with your Mexican cheese
- Place this in the oven and bake for 10 minutes
- Serve with cilantro and sour cream and have your bliss moment!

Greek meatballs with Avocado Tzatziki sauce

Don't let the exotic name fool you. This is among my favorite meatball recipes and with good reason. It's quite easy to prepare, and you can always choose whether to use beef or lamb meat for the meatballs.

Mostly I use whatever meat I have in the kitchen between the two, and I end up getting the same sumptuous result.

You can always pair the meatballs with a salad and use the sauce as a dressing, or you can have the meatballs with the sauce as dip, which is what I do.

Preparation time: 30 minutes

Serves: 4

Ingredients:

- **For the Avocado Tzatziki**
- Avocado, ripe and sliced – 2
- Garlic, crushed – 3 cloves
- Medium sized cucumber, diced – 1
- Red onion, chopped – 1
- Lemon juice – 1 tablespoon
- Fresh mint leaves, shredded – ½ cup
- Greek yogurt – 1/3 cup
- Sea salt and freshly crushed black pepper to sample

For the Greek meatballs

- Lamb or beef, Ground- 2 lb.
- Garlic, crushed – 3 cloves
- Red onion, chopped – 1/3 cup
- Lemon zest – ¼ cup
- Ground coriander – ½ tablespoon
- Ground cumin – 1 teaspoon

- Fresh oregano, shredded – 2 tablespoons
- Sea salt and black pepper to taste

Method:

- Preheat your oven to 350 degrees F
- Mix all your Greek meatball ingredients together and form 2 inch balls each
- Line your baking pan with nonstick spray and bake for up to 25 minutes. Set aside
- Add all your Tzatziki ingredients in a food processor. Blend until it forms a smooth texture
- Serve with the Greek meatballs

Enjoy!

Avocado Caprese skillet chicken

I love chicken, and if I could, I would have it every day with my meals. This particular recipe is so simple you can prepare for dinner after a long day. It takes less than 30 minutes to create this magical chicken and avocado combo.

You can even grill the chicken instead of going the skillet way. It's completely up to you. However, I like frying my chicken since it allows all the flavors to mix perfectly. This allows you to taste each flavor as you eat.

Preparation time: 25 minutes

Serves: 4

Ingredients:

- Avocado, peeled and sliced – 2
- Chicken breasts, boneless, butterflied and halved – 24 oz
- Onion powder – 1 teaspoon
- Garlic, crushed – 2 cloves
- Extra virgin olive oil – 2 tablespoons
- Italian seasoning – 1 teaspoon
- Ripe tomatoes, Well diced – 2
- Kosher salt and pepper
- Fresh mozzarella, nicely cut- 8pieces
- Balsamic glaze – 2 tablespoons
- Fresh basil, shredded – ¼ cup

Method:

- Combine onion powder, crushed garlic, Italian seasoning, pepper and salt in a large bowl

- Coat both sides of your chicken with this mixture
- Using a big pan, heat the olive oil over medium-high heat and then immerse the chicken
- Brown both sides of the chicken. This should only take about 3 minutes each side or until well cooked
- Add your mozzarella slices on the fried chicken, topping it with the avocado slices and finally tomato slices
- Cover your pan and keep cooking for an extra 2 minutes
- Remove pan from heat and season with black pepper, balsamic glaze, basil and serve while hot.

Enjoy!

Pan-seared salmon with creamy avocado sauce

I always say that a fish dish should always be kept very simple. This is precisely why this pan-seared salmon recipe is just the perfect fit for those days you are craving fish. The avocado sauce brings a healthy and creamy twist to the whole meal which is hard to ignore.

Preparation time: 20 minutes

Serves: 4

Ingredients:

- Salmon fillets, skinless – 28 oz.
- Extra virgin olive oil - 3 tablespoons
- Kosher salt and black pepper to taste
- Fresh basil, shredded, to garnish – ¼ cup
- Lemon wedges - 4

For the avocado sauce

- Ripe avocado, peeled and halved – 2
- Garlic, crushed – 2 cloves
- Fresh basil leaves, shredded – ½ cup
- Extra virgin olive oil – 1/3 cup
- Lemon juice, Freshly squeezed–2 tablespoons
- Cream of your choice – 3 tablespoons
- Kosher salt and freshly ground black pepper to taste

Method:

- Start by combining the avocado sauce ingredients in a blender. Blend until your desired consistency and set aside
- Use the kosher salt and pepper to season your salmon
- In a large skillet, add your extra virgin olive oil and heat over medium- high heat

- Add your salmon fillets when the oil is hot and sear for 5 minutes each on each side
- Remove the cooked fillets from heat and sprinkle the avocado sauce on them
- Garnish with basil and serve while hot, with lemon wedges.

Enjoy!

Avocado and lump crab

You have guests coming over, or it's your turn to host the monthly book club, and you just have no idea what to make for dinner.

Well, why not try this lump crab with an avocado recipe? It's an exciting dish that you will enjoy preparing, in less than 30 minutes and your guests will be asking for more.

Preparation time: 20 minutes

Serves: 6

Ingredients:

- Ripe avocado, peeled and halved – 3
- Lump crab meat, cooked or canned – 12oz.
- Red onion, nicely chopped – 2
- Cherry tomatoes, diced – 3
- Fresh basil leaves, shredded – ½ cup
- Extra virgin olive oil – 2 tablespoons
- Lemon juice – 3 tablespoons
- Butter lettuce, chopped - 2
- Kosher salt and black pepper to taste

Method:

- Mix your chopped red onions, basil, cherry tomatoes, lime juice, olive oil, kosher salt and black pepper in a large bowl
- Toss in your crab meat and mix gently
- Take your halved avocados and scoop all the avocado out
- Transfer the crab mixture to the empty avocado halves
- Garnish with lettuce and serve

CHAPTER 4: DESSERTS AND SMOOTHIES WITH AVOCADO

I work out a lot. The last thing I want is to fill up on unhealthy foods during or after my workouts, which are plenty intense. I always go for avocado smoothies which are not only creamy and delicious but also have fiber that my body needs.

The desserts with avocado will simply delight you and your family with their mouthwatering taste. My family loves the desserts so much, especially for ice cream. If you have a sweet tooth, this is for you. You can now curb those cravings with a healthier option.

Avocado and banana ice-cream

Ice-cream just got more delicious and healthier. The avocados bring healthy fats to the menu while the bananas bring the sweetness and fiber that is vital for proper nutrition.

Preparation time: 7 minutes

Serves: 4

Ingredients:

- Ripe Avocado, cut into pieces - 1
- Ripe bananas, sliced into bits and frozen overnight – 4
- Pure vanilla extract – 1 tablespoon

- Natural cane sugar (optional)
- Sprinkles – a handful

Method:

- Combine your pieces of avocado, vanilla extract, and sliced bananas in a food processor for about 3 minutes. Do not add any liquids under any circumstance. Give the mixture a bit of time to come together.
- Serve over sprinkles and enjoy.

Paleo chocolate mousse

Having gone paleo for a while now, this fine mousse was a must-make. We all love chocolate, and this is just a healthier way to have it when the cravings kick in. You can freeze the mousse and have it whenever you want. It tastes just like ice-cream.

Preparation time: 18 minutes

Serves: 4

Ingredients:

- Avocados, peeled and cut in half – 3
- Natural Honey – ¼ cup

- Unsweetened cacao powder – ¾ cup
- Almond coconut milk – ½ cup
- Sea salt – a pinch

Method:

- Merge all your ingredients in a blender or a food processor, whichever you have in your household. They all work well with this.
- Blend the mixture until it gets a smooth texture
- Transfer the mixture to an airtight container and store in the refrigerator for an hour or until you are ready to serve

Serve and enjoy!

Avocado brownies

The exclusive thing you will need to change from your brownie routine is to make them healthier by replacing the oil you use and butter with avocados. I have tried different brownie recipes, but this is the best so far.

Make sure to use Dutch processed cacao powder as instructed to have sweet brownies.

Preparation time: 40 minutes

Serves: 6

Ingredients:

- Ripe large avocados, sliced – 3
- Eggs – 4
- Coconut flour – ¾ cup
- Natural Coconut Oil – ½ cup
- Unsweetened applesauce – ½ cup
- Maple Syrup – ½ cup
- Vanilla extract – ½ tablespoon
- Unsweetened Dutch processed cacao powder – ¾ cup
- Sea salt – 1/3 teaspoon
- Baking soda – 1 tablespoon

Method:

- Start by preheating your oven up to 350 degrees F
- Add your avocados, maple syrup, applesauce and vanilla extract in a blender or food processor and mix until it forms a thick consistency (you can mix using your hands, but it takes longer)
- Transfer the mixture to a large bowl. After that, immediately add eggs and whisk
- Stir in your coconut flour, cacao powder, sea salt and baking soda

- Use natural coconut oil to grease your baking pan
- Add the batter and bake for 30 minutes
- Take it out from the oven, set aside to cool for 30 minutes then cut into 18 pieces or more
- Store it in an airtight container. This is until you are ready to serve. For the brownies to last longer, store in the refrigerator

Enjoy!

Pineapple Avocado ultimate green smoothie

This is always my go-to smoothie when I'm in a rush, and I'm in dire need of a sweet energy boost. Not only does it take fewer ingredients, but it also tastes great.

You can never go wrong when making this. The trick is always to add your frozen ingredients last when making smoothies. The liquids should come first.

Preparation time: 10 minutes

Serves: 4

Ingredients:

- Ripe avocado, peeled and pitted – 2
- Pineapple, sliced and frozen – 3 cups
- Water – 2 cups
- Kale, shredded – 1 ½ cups
- Natural Honey to taste – 2 tablespoons

Method:

- Add water to your blender. Next, add your avocado, kale and pineapple should be on top.
- Blend to your desired consistency
- Stir in the honey and blend until it's well mixed
- Turn off the blender and serve

Layered avocado and strawberry smoothie

Wondering what to make during one of those hot days? This smoothie is an interesting pick that looks fantastic with the strawberry and avocado layers. The taste is one to die for especially because it's sweet and refreshing at the same time. Just perfect for a sunny day on the patio.

If you are vegan, substitute the honey with agave nectar. Both ways work perfectly.

Preparation time: 10 minutes

Serves: 4

Ingredients:

For the avocado smoothie

- Ripe avocado, chopped – 2
- Unsweetened almond milk – ½ cup
- Natural honey to taste – 3 tablespoons
- Pure vanilla extract – ½ tablespoon
- Lemon juice – 3 teaspoons
- Ice cubes – ½ cup

For the strawberry smoothie

- Frozen strawberries, unthawed – 2 cups
- Water – ¾ cup
- Frozen banana, sliced into bits – 1
- Natural honey – 2 teaspoons
- Lemon juice – 2 teaspoons

Method:

- Add all the avocado smoothie ingredients in a blender and blend until you get a smooth mixture
- Transfer this mixture to glasses. Pour halfway to each glass, and store in the freezer
- Clean the blender and add your strawberry smoothie ingredients and blend until it attains a smooth texture
- Gently pour your strawberry smoothie to fill up the glasses with the avocado smoothie

Dazzling Pineapple Cookbook:

An Ultimate Collection of 25 Pinelicious Recipes

Table of Content

INTRODUCTION 1
INTRODUCTION 8
CHAPTER 1: APPETIZERS AND DIPS WITH AVOCADO 9
    Crispy baked avocado fries 10
    Avocado egg rolls with sweet chili sauce 13
    Sweet potato guacamole bacon bites 16
    Avocado dip with corn 19
    Avocado bomb sauce 21
    Creamy avocado ranch dip 24
    The ultimate green avocado spinach dip 27
CHAPTER 2: SALADS AND VEGAN MEALS WITH AVOCADO 30
    Avocado and three bean salad 31
    Avocado tuna salad 34
    Avocado egg salad 36
    Cucumber, tomato and avocado salad 38
    Vegan potato salad with cilantro and dill 40
    Avocado Chickpea with vegan pesto 43
    Black bean salad with avocado cilantro- lime juice 45
CHAPTER 3: MAIN COURSE MEALS WITH AVOCADO 48
    Steak and sweet potato bowls with avocado cilantro drizzle 48
    Stuffed avocado tacos 54
    Greek meatballs with Avocado Tzatziki sauce 57
    Avocado Caprese skillet chicken 60
    Pan-seared salmon with creamy avocado sauce 63
    Avocado and lump crab 66
CHAPTER 4: DESSERTS AND SMOOTHIES WITH AVOCADO 69
    Avocado and banana ice-cream 69
    Paleo chocolate mousse 72

Avocado brownies 75

Pineapple Avocado ultimate green smoothie 78

Layered avocado and strawberry smoothie 80

Chapter 1: Delicious Pineapple Smoothies & Breakfasts 88

Morning Pineapple Flax 88

Pineapple Egg Toast 90

Morning Pineapple Oat Granola Mix 92

Truly Tropical Mango Pineapple Smoothie 94

Pineapple Orange Smoothie 96

Pineapple Honey Peach Smoothie 97

Chapter 2: Fresh Pineapple Meals & Salads 99

Wholesome Pineapple Avocado Corn Salad 99

Fruity Pineapple Yogurt Salad 101

Pork Pineapple Rice Treat 103

Pineapple Berry Kale Salad 105

Pineapple Mayo Chicken Salad 107

Pineapple Glazed Pork Roast 109

Salmon Pineapple Meal 112

BBQ Pineapple Chicken 114

Chapter 3: Popular Pinelicious Recipes 116

Pineapple Perky Sandwich 116

Pineapple Rum Relish 118

Pineapple Tortilla Pizza 120

Shrimp Pineapple Zucchini Curry 122

Cinnamon Pineapple Bites 124

Chapter 4: Awesome Pineapple Desserts 126

Pineapple Cream Cake 126

Pineapple Ginger Sorbet 128

Pineapple Marshmallow Fluff 130

Pineapple Dessert Cookies 132

Pineapple Cheese Casserole 134
Pineapple Fruit Freeze 136
Conclusion 138

Introduction

The tropical aroma of Pineapple is too good to let go every time you take a knife and slice it. Pineapples are so delicious that you hardly ever find someone who doesn't like its exquisite flavor no matter where you travel across the Mother Earth. This tropical fruit is highly satisfying and can be enjoyed in various creative ways to have a guilt-free pleasure. In addition, it is so easy to include it in cooking and you will be surprised to know how many meals you can use them in. Alternatively, you can just simply make the most out of its tangy flavor by slicing and enjoy it solo or with your favorite fruit dip.

And though pineapple's taste is the best when it is freshly-sliced, it is one of those rare fruits that can be enjoyed all year long, at any season and either fresh or preserved or even sun dried.

Pineapple is a Superfood

One awesome thing about the Pineapple is that it contains very few calories and is rich in minerals and vitamins. Pineapple is a magnificent source of disease fighting anti-oxidants, vitamin C and vitamin A, keeping you safe from being vulnerable to harmful diseases and infections. This tropical fruit is fully-loaded with copper, manganese and potassium to ensure healthy body functions.

In addition, the high contents of Bromelain, which is said to help in weight control, make the pineapple a perfect pick for ensuring optimal wellness and fitness, helping maintain a truly healthy lifestyle.

Pineapple is a versatile fruit as well, and can be used not only to prepare fresh juices and smoothies, but it can also be a main ingredient in your favorite pizzas, salads, desserts, breakfasts, and main course meals. This cookbook unveils a thoroughly-picked collection of 25 exclusive Pineapple recipes to enjoy with your family, including refreshing pineapple salads, delicious pineapple smoothies, scrumptious pineapple main meals and of course, amazing pineapple desserts

Get ready to explore the vibrant recipes featuring this super fruit and surprise your family with its tangiest flavors.

Chapter 1: Delicious Pineapple Smoothies & Breakfasts

Morning Pineapple Flax

Prep Time: 20 min.

Serves: 2-3

Ingredients:

- 1 cup pineapple, diced
- 1 cup Greek yogurt
- ½ almond extract

- 1 tbs. flaxseeds
- 1/3 cup almond milk

Directions:

- In a bowl of medium size, thoroughly mix the almond milk and yogurt.

- Add the extract and flaxseeds, and mix well.

- Serve in two bowls – diced pineapple at the bottom, then add a layer of yoghurt mix, top with flaxseeds and another layer of yoghurt

- Enjoy with your family.

Pineapple Egg Toast

Prep Time: 20 min.

Serves: 3-4

Ingredients:

- 6 eggs
- 1 minced cloves garlic
- 1 tbs. whole milk
- ½ tsp. chili powder
- ½ diced pineapple
- 1/2 chopped red bell pepper
- ½ cup Swiss cheese, shredded
- Pepper and salt as needed
- 1 tbs. unsalted butter

Directions:

- Take a skillet of medium size and add in the butter; heat the pan over medium heat.

- Add the pepper and garlic; cook for a few minutes. Set aside.

- In a bowl of medium size, thoroughly whisk the eggs, milk, cheese, chili powder, salt, and pepper.

- Add the cooked vegetables and pineapple to the eggs mixture.

- Cook the egg mixture, constantly stirring until it turns scrambled.

- Serve the eggs with toast.

Morning Pineapple Oat Granola Mix

Prep Time: 15-20 min.

Serves: 2-3

Ingredients:

- ½ cup rolled oats
- 2 tbs. maple syrup
- 2 tbs. orange juice
- 1 cup pineapple, diced
- 2 tbs. coconut oil
- ¼ cup shredded coconut
- ¼ cup pecans

Directions:

- Take a skillet of medium size and add in the oil; heat the pan over medium heat.

- Add the maple syrup, and orange juice. Heat the mixture.

- Mix the oats, coconut, pecans, and pineapple.

- Cook for 8-10 minutes.

- Serve this warm pineapple breakfast on top of the cheese or plain yogurt (optional).

Truly Tropical Mango Pineapple Smoothie

Prep Time: 5 min.

Serves: 2

Ingredients:

- 1/2 cup vanilla yogurt

- 1/4 cup coconut cream
- 1 cup mango
- 1 tbs. flax seed, ground
- 1/2 cup pineapple

Directions:

- In a blender or food processor, one by one add all the ingredients. Blend or process on pulse mode until your smoothie is well-combined.

- Add more ice if needed to make it extra chilled.

- Pour the pineapple smoothie in a tall glass or Mason jar and serve chilled.

- Decorate with a slice of pineapple on the glass rim (optional).

Pineapple Orange Smoothie

Prep Time: 5 min.

Serves: 2

Ingredients:

- 1/2 cup orange juice
- 1 1/2 cups vanilla yogurt
- 2 cups pineapple chunks
- 2 cups strawberries

Directions:

- In a blender or food processor, one by one add all the ingredients. Blend or process on pulse mode until well-combined.

- Add more ice if needed to make it extra chilled.

- Pour the pineapple smoothie in a smoothie glass and serve chilled.

- Decorate the glass rim with a slice of orange (optional).

Pineapple Honey Peach Smoothie

Prep Time: 5-8 min.

Serves: 2

Ingredients:

- 1/2 tsp. vanilla extract
- 1 cup almond milk, unsweetened

- 1/2 cup peach slices
- 1/2 cup plain yogurt
- 1/2 cup pineapple chunks
- 1 tbs. honey
- ½ banana

Directions:

- In a blender or food processor, one by one add all the ingredients. Blend or process on pulse mode until well-combined.

- Add more ice if needed to make it extra chilled.

- Pour the pineapple smoothie in a Mason jar or smoothie glass and serve chilled.

- Decorate with a slice of pineapple or strawberry (optional).

Chapter 2: Fresh Pineapple Meals & Salads

Wholesome Pineapple Avocado Corn Salad

Prep Time: 8-10 min.

Serves: 5-6

Ingredients:

- 1 medium jalapeno, chopped
- 3/4 cup cucumber, diced
- 1 1/4 cups pineapple, diced
- 1/2 cup cilantro, chopped
- 2 ears corn, separate kernels
- 1 tsp. honey
- 3/4 cup onion, diced
- 1 large avocado, peeled and diced
- 3 tbs. lime juice
- 1/4 tsp. kosher salt

Directions:

- In a bowl of small size, thoroughly mix the lime juice, honey, and salt.

- In a bowl of medium size, thoroughly mix the all remaining ingredients and toss well.

- Pour the lime mixture over salad and toss well.

- Serve the salad fresh.

Fruity Pineapple Yogurt Salad

Prep Time: 8-10 min.

Serves: 2-3

Ingredients:

- 1 cup strawberries, cut into slices
- 1/3 cup orange juice
- 3/4 cup milk
- 11 oz can oranges, drained
- 1 cup vanilla yogurt
- 20 oz. can pineapple tidbits
- 2 bananas, sliced
- 3.5 oz. instant vanilla pudding mix

Directions:

- In a bowl of medium size, thoroughly mix the orange juice, milk, and pudding mix.

- Beat the mixture well using a hand blender for 2 minutes.

- Mix the yogurt, pineapple, strawberries, oranges, and bananas.

- Serve the salad fresh.

Pork Pineapple Rice Treat

Prep Time: 35-40 min.

Serves: 4-5

Ingredients:

- 2 cups diced pineapple
- 1 small chopped carrot
- 4 cups vegetable broth
- 2 cups brown rice
- 2 minced cloves garlic
- 2 cups cooked diced pork
- 3 tbs. soy sauce

- 1 small yellow onion, chopped
- 1 cup sweet peas
- 1 tbs. peanut oil
- Pepper and salt as needed
- ½ tsp. ginger powder

Directions:

- Take a saucepan of medium size and add in the broth; heat the pan over medium heat.

- Boil the broth and cook the rice according to directions.

- Drain well and set the rice aside.

- Take a skillet of medium size and add in the peanut oil; heat the pan over medium heat.

- Cook the garlic, onion, and carrot for 8-10 minutes.

- In a bowl of medium size, thoroughly mix the soy sauce, ginger, salt, pepper, and more peanut oil.

- Add the oil mixture to the skillet and continue cooking for 1 minute.

- Add the peas, pork, cooked rice, and pineapple.

- Cook for 8-10 minutes and serve warm!

Pineapple Berry Kale Salad

Prep Time: 10-12 min.

Serves: 2

Ingredients:

- 1/2 cup blueberries
- 1/4 cup salad dressing
- 1/2 cup pineapple, chopped

- 2 tbs. feta cheese, crumbled
- 4 cups kale leaves, chopped

Directions:

- In a bowl of medium size, thoroughly mix the kale and dressing for about 3 minutes.

- Combine until the kale wilts perfectly.

- On top add the cheese, blueberries, and pineapple.

- Serve the salad fresh.

Pineapple Mayo Chicken Salad

Prep Time: 8-10 min.

Serves: 2-3

Ingredients:

- ½ cup chopped pineapple
- ½ cup thinly sliced green onions
- ½ tsp. finely shredded lemon peel
- ¼ cup macadamia nuts, chopped
- ¼ tsp. salt

- ½ cup chopped celery
- 1 tsp. snipped fresh basil
- 1/3 cup low-fat mayonnaise
- 1 cup cooked chicken, chopped
- Bread slices or mixed salad greens (optional)

Directions:

- In a bowl of medium size, thoroughly mix the chicken, celery, onions, and chopped pineapple.

- In another bowl of small size, thoroughly mix the mayonnaise, basil, salt, and lemon peel.

- Top the mayo mix over the chicken mixture.

- Toss well; cover and chill for 2-4 hours.

- Take out, top with the macadamia nuts.

- Serve and enjoy.

Pineapple Glazed Pork Roast

Prep Time: 40-50 min.

Serves: 10-12

Ingredients:

- ¾ cup orange juice
- 10oz can pineapple rings
- 1 tsp. oregano, ground
- 5 garlic cloves, peeled
- 1 tsp. cumin, ground
- 2 tbs. olive oil
- 2 tbs. orange zest
- ¼ cup lime juice
- ¼ cup pure honey
- ½ cup pineapple juice
- 5 to 6-pound pork shoulder, trimmed, fat removed

Directions:

- Add ¼ cup orange juice, lime juice, and pineapple juice in a food processor.

- Add the zest and 2-3 pineapple rings; process on pulse mode for a few seconds.

- Add another ¼ cup orange juice; combine and add the garlic cumin, oregano, and olive oil.

- Process on pulse mode to combine.

- Puncture pork shoulder all over using a fork so that juices can be absorbed.

- Arrange the pork in a large bowl and pour the fruit marinade. Rub the meat well.

- Refrigerate and marinate for 2-3 hours; turn the marinade in between.

- Preheat an oven to 325 degrees F.

- Arrange the pork on a rack in a roasting pan.

- Roast for about 65-70 minutes.

- In a blender, combine remaining ¼ cup orange juice with honey.

- Take out the pork and baste it several times to create a glaze. Add the remaining pineapple rings.

- Cook the pork for 20 more minutes or until internal thermometer reads 140 to 165 degrees.

- Slice and serve with cooked rice.

Salmon Pineapple Meal

Prep Time: 35-40 min.

Serves: 4-5

Ingredients:

- 1 cup diced tomatoes
- 2 tbs. cilantro, fresh chopped
- 2 tbs. lemon juice
- 3 tbs. honey
- 3 tbs. worcestershire sauce
- 4 medium size salmon filets
- 1 cups diced pineapple
- Pepper and salt as needed
- Smoked paprika

Directions:

- Preheat the oven to 400 °F.

- Grease a large baking dish with some cooking spray.

- In a bowl of medium size, thoroughly mix the tomatoes, pineapple, lemon juice, honey, sauce, cilantro, and seasonings.

- Now season the fish with salt and pepper.

- Arrange the salmon on the baking dish and top the fillets with the pineapple mixture.

- Bake for 20-35 minutes.

- Serve with cooked long grain rice.

BBQ Pineapple Chicken

Prep Time: 25-30 min.

Serves: 4

Ingredients:

- 2 tbs. honey BBQ sauce
- 1 ½ cup cooked chicken, shredded
- 1 pitted and diced avocado

- ½ cup diced pineapple
- 2 tbs. coconut oil
- ½ cup or more as needed sharp cheddar cheese, shredded
- 4 small–medium tortillas

Directions:

- In a bowl of medium size, thoroughly mix the chicken with the BBQ sauce.

- Arrange the tortilla, divide the chicken, pineapple, avocado, and shredded cheese.

- Take a skillet of medium size and add in the oil; heat the pan over medium heat.

- Fold the quesadillas in half. Cook them on both sides for a few minutes.

- Top them with sour cream (optional) and serve warm!

Chapter 3: Popular Pinelicious Recipes

Pineapple Perky Sandwich

Prep Time: 10-15 min.

Serves: 4

Ingredients:

- 12 slices cooked ham, sliced
- 2 tsp. butter
- ½ cup (4 ounces) cream cheese
- 8 slices of whole-wheat bread
- 4 large slices of pineapple

Directions:

- Spread the cheese on the bread slices.

- Layer each slices with a pineapple ring, and ham.

- Top with remaining bread slice.

- Take a skillet of medium size and add in the butter; heat the pan over medium heat.

- Heat the sandwiches for 3-4 minutes on each side or until they turn light brown. Press with a spatula.

- Serve warm with your favorite sandwich sauce or dip!

Pineapple Rum Relish

Prep Time: 10 min.

Serves: 4-5

Ingredients:

- ½ cup finely chopped yellow onion
- 1 cup peeled and chopped mango
- 1 red bell pepper, seeded and finely diced
- ¼ cup scallions, finely diced
- 1 tbs. granulated sugar
- ¼ cup golden rum
- 1 ripe pineapple, peeled and make small pieces

- 2 tbs. sherry vinegar

Directions:

- Take a saucepan of medium size and add in the vinegar and sugar; heat the pan over medium heat.

- Add the pineapple, mango, onion, and pepper; simmer the mixture for about 2-3 minutes.

- Add the scallions and rum; combine well.

- Cook for another 4 minutes.

- Serve warm or after cooling!

Pineapple Tortilla Pizza

Prep Time: 10-15 min.

Serves: 3-4

Ingredients:

- 1 large whole wheat tortilla
- 1/4 cup mozzarella cheese, grated
- 1/4 cup pineapple tidbits

- 1/4 cup ham slices
- 1/4 cup tomato pizza sauce

Directions:

- Preheat an oven to 350 degree F.

- Add the tortilla on baking sheet then spread pizza sauce.

- Top with the ham slices, cheese, and pineapple.

- Bake the pizza for 8-10 minutes or until the edges become light brown.

- Serve and enjoy.

Shrimp Pineapple Zucchini Curry

Prep Time: 25-30 min.

Serves: 3-4

Ingredients:

- 2 tbs. cilantro, chopped
- 1 zucchini, diced
- 1 pound large shrimp, peeled and deveined
- 2 tbs. basil, chopped
- 3 tbs. fish sauce
- 1 medium banana, sliced
- 1 cup coconut milk
- 1 1/2 cups pineapple, diced
- 1/2 cup curry paste
- 2 tbs. vegetable oil

Directions:

- Add the banana, fish sauce, and milk into the blender and blend until smooth.

- Take a saucepan of medium size and add in the oil; heat the pan over medium heat.

- Add the curry paste and stir for 2 minutes.

- Add the pineapple and cook for 2 minutes. Set the mixture aside.

- Add the shrimp in the pan and sauté till pink; set aside the shrimp mixture.

- Add the milk mixture over pineapples and stir well.

- Add in the pan and cook for another 3 minutes.

- Add the zucchini and cook for another 2 minutes.

- Add the shrimp to the pan and stir well.

- Top with the fresh herbs and serve warm!

Cinnamon Pineapple Bites

Prep Time: 15-20 min.

Serves: 4-5

Ingredients:

- 12 oz. pineapples chunks

- 4 tsp. coconut oil
- 1/2 tsp. cinnamon
- 2 tbs. honey
- Crème cheese or vanilla ice-cream for garnishing

Directions:

- Preheat your grill.

- In a bowl of medium size, thoroughly mix the cinnamon and honey.

- Tear the foil into four squares and place one tsp. of oil on each foil.

- Add the pineapples in the four foil squares.

- Top with the honey and cinnamon.

- Fold packet tightly and grill for 8-10 minutes.

- Serve warm topped with cream cheese or ice-cream!

Chapter 4: Awesome Pineapple Desserts

Pineapple Cream Cake

Prep Time: 35-40 min.

Serves: 4

Ingredients:

- 1 cup brown sugar
- 2 cups coconut flour
- 1 cup apple sauce
- Pinch salt

- 2 medium eggs
- 1 can pineapple, crushed
- 1 tsp. vanilla

For Icing:

- 2 cups confectioner's sugar
- 1 tsp. vanilla
- 1 pack cream cheese (room temperature)
- 3 tbs. coconut oil
- Optional: shredded coconut

Directions:

- Preheat the oven to 375 degree F.

- Grease a square baking dish with some cooking spray.

- In a bowl of medium size, thoroughly mix the coconut flour, brown sugar, and salt.

- Mix the vanilla, eggs, and applesauce; combine well.

- Mix in the crushed pineapple.

- Add the batter into the baking dish and bake for 35-40 minutes.

- In a bowl of medium size, thoroughly whisk the cheese, coconut oil, confectioner's sugar, and vanilla.

- Top the cake with the cheese icing. Sprinkle the cake with some shredded coconut (optional).

Pineapple Ginger Sorbet

Prep Time: 5 min.

Serves: 3-4

Ingredients:

- 1 tbs. lemon juice or orange juice
- 1 tbs. ginger, grated
- ½ cup pineapple juice
- 1 cup granulated sugar
- 2 cups light cream

Directions:

- In a bowl of medium size, thoroughly mix the ingredients.

- Place in a freezer until partially frozen.

- Whisk with a wooden spoon every 40-50 minutes.

- Return to the freezer until completely frozen. Serve chilled!

- Garnish with pineapple slice and cherry.

Pineapple Marshmallow Fluff

Prep Time: 8-10 min.

Serves: 8-10

Ingredients:

- 2 cups marshmallows
- 8 oz. cool whip, thawed
- 20 oz. can pineapple, crushed
- 1 cup coconut, shredded & sweetened
- 3 1/2 oz. vanilla instant pudding mix

Directions:

- In a bowl of medium size, thoroughly mix the pineapple and pudding mix.

- Add the coconut, marshmallows, and cool whip. Combine well.

- Cover bowl with a lid and add in refrigerator for 2-3 hours.

- Serve chilled!

Pineapple Dessert Cookies

Prep Time: 25-30 min.

Serves: Makes 50-55 cookies

Ingredients:

- 3/4 cup pineapple, crushed and drained
- 1/2 tsp. almond extract
- 2/3 cup shortening
- 2 tsp. baking powder
- 1 egg
- 1/2 cup shredded coconut
- 1 1/4 cup sugar
- 2 cups all-purpose flour
- 1/2 tsp. salt

Directions:

- Preheat the oven to 325 degree F.

- In a bowl of medium size, thoroughly mix the flour, salt, and baking powder.

- In another bowl of medium size, thoroughly mix the shortening, almond extract, and sugar.

- Add egg and beat until turn fluffy.

- Mix both mixtures and add the pineapple; combine well.

- Add 1 tsp. full of cookie dough onto a greased baking tray; top with shredded coconut.

- Bake for 18-20 minutes or until lightly brown. Serve warm!

Pineapple Cheese Casserole

Prep Time: 40-45 min.

Serves: 5-6

Ingredients:

- 2 cups pineapple, chopped
- 3/4 cup coconut palm sugar
- 2 tbs. lemon juice
- 1/4 cup coconut flour
- 1 cup panko breadcrumb
- 1/2 cup butter,
- 1 cup chard cheese, shredded
- Pinch cinnamon

Directions:

- Preheat the oven to 375 degrees F.

- Grease a baking dish using some cooking spray.

- In a bowl of medium size, thoroughly mix the flour with the breadcrumbs, butter and sharp cheddar.

- In the greased baking dish, arrange the pineapple in the bottom and pour the lemon juice on top.

- Add the palm sugar all over and then the cinnamon.

- Top with the prepared topping evenly and bake for about 30 minutes or until it turns light brown.

- Serve the casserole warm!

Pineapple Fruit Freeze

Prep Time: 8-10 min.

Serves: 4-5

- ¼ cup peach nectar or your favorite juice
- ¾ cup pineapple, diced

- ¾ cup peaches, peeled and diced
- ¾ cup banana, sliced
- ¾ cup mango, peeled and diced
- ¾ cup papaya, peeled and diced
- 1 tablespoon honey
- ½ cup crushed ice

Directions:

- Blend everything in your blender to make a perfectly smooth mixture. Add more ice if needed.

- Add in freezer safe glasses or use ice-cream molds to make fruit ice.

- Freeze for a few hours to make it thick (optional) or serve right away as a smoothie.

Conclusion

I would like to thank you for buying and getting to the end of my new book, ***Fruitilicious! 50 Super Delicious Avocado and Pineapple Recipes***

Could you ever imagine you can make so many diverse meals featuring Pineapple and Avocado? There are countless options since these tropical fruits are so versatile and capable to add an exotic note to any of your meals, be it a main dish or just a morning smoothie.

I sincerely hope that the book has succeeded in its aim to provide the readers with the most unusual and creative ways to enjoy the Pineapple and avocado, helping you make some heavenly delicious meals at home and enjoy with your family.

Finally, if you enjoyed this cookbook, will please take a few minutes of your valuable time to leave a short honest review. It would be greatly appreciated and will help me work on improving my books in the future!

Thank you and have a great time enjoying the delicious recipes!

Keep cooking healthy food and living a healthy life!

With Love,

Robert Pratt

Text Copyright © Robert Pratt

All rights reserved. No part of this guide may be reproduced in any form without permission in writing from the publisher except in the case of brief quotations embodied in critical articles or reviews.

Legal & Disclaimer

The information contained in this book and its contents is not designed to replace or take the place of any form of medical or professional advice; and is not meant to replace the need for independent medical, financial, legal or other professional advice or services, as may be required. The content and information in this book has been provided for educational and entertainment purposes only.

The content and information contained in this book has been compiled from sources deemed reliable, and it is accurate to the best of the Author's knowledge, information and belief. However, the Author cannot guarantee its accuracy and validity and cannot be held liable for any errors and/or omissions. Further, changes are periodically made to this book as and when needed. Where appropriate and/or necessary, you must consult a professional (including but not limited to your doctor, attorney, financial advisor or such other professional advisor) before using any of the suggested remedies, techniques, or information in this book.

Upon using the contents and information contained in this book, you agree to hold harmless the Author from and against any damages, costs, and expenses, including any legal fees potentially resulting from the application of any of the information provided by this book. This disclaimer applies to any loss, damages or injury caused by the use and application, whether directly or indirectly, of any advice or information presented, whether for breach of contract, tort, negligence, personal injury, criminal intent, or under any other cause of action.

You agree to accept all risks of using the information presented inside this book.

You agree that by continuing to read this book, where appropriate and/or necessary, you shall consult a professional (including but not limited to your doctor, attorney, or financial advisor or such other advisor as needed) before using any of the suggested remedies, techniques, or information in this book.

CPSIA information can be obtained
at www.ICGtesting.com
Printed in the USA
FSHW012053261118
54056FS